Presenting:

PURPLE ZURPLE

A ROYAL COLOR UNLIKE ANY OTHER!

WORDS & ART BY: BRIANNA DAVIS

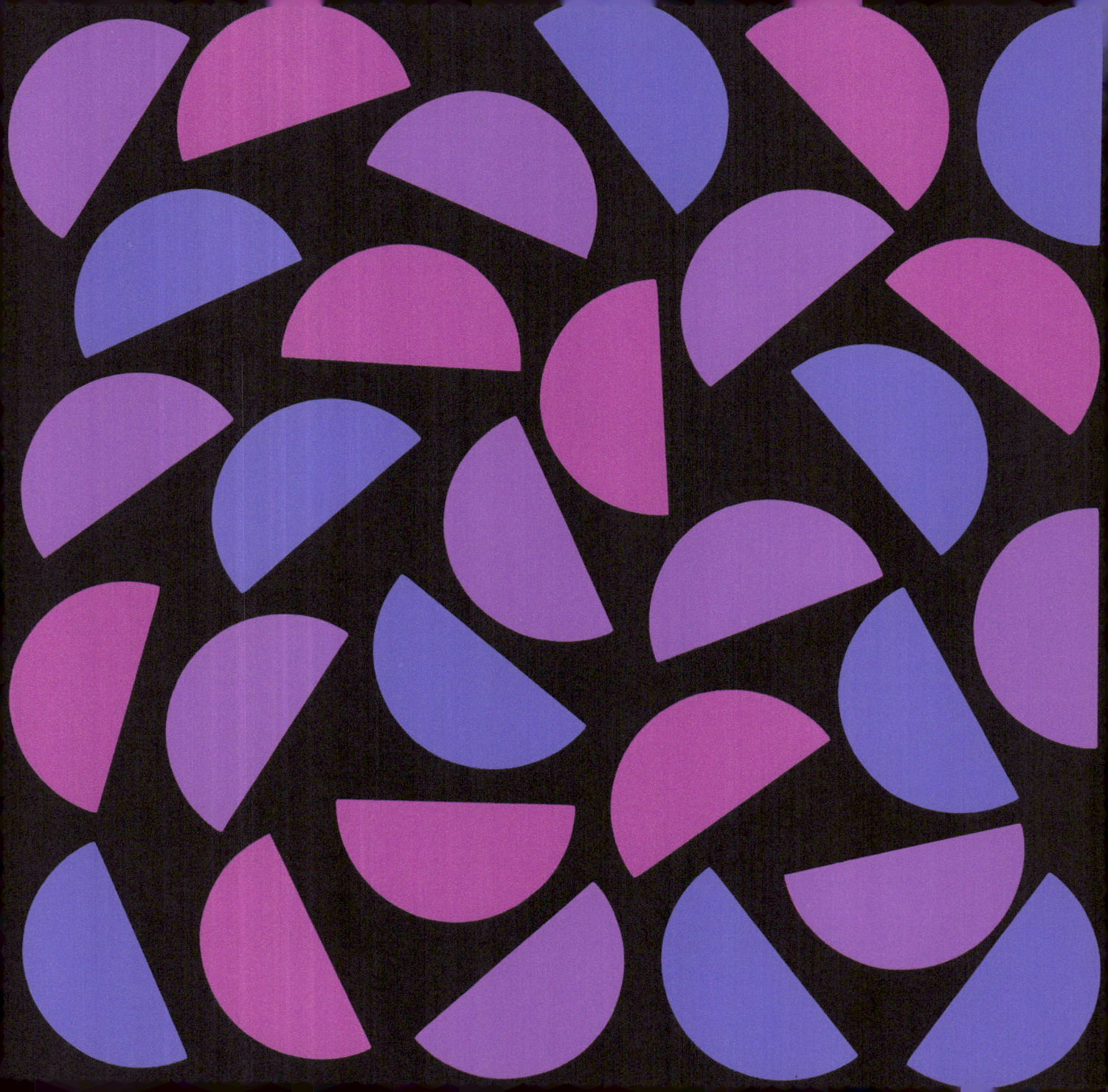

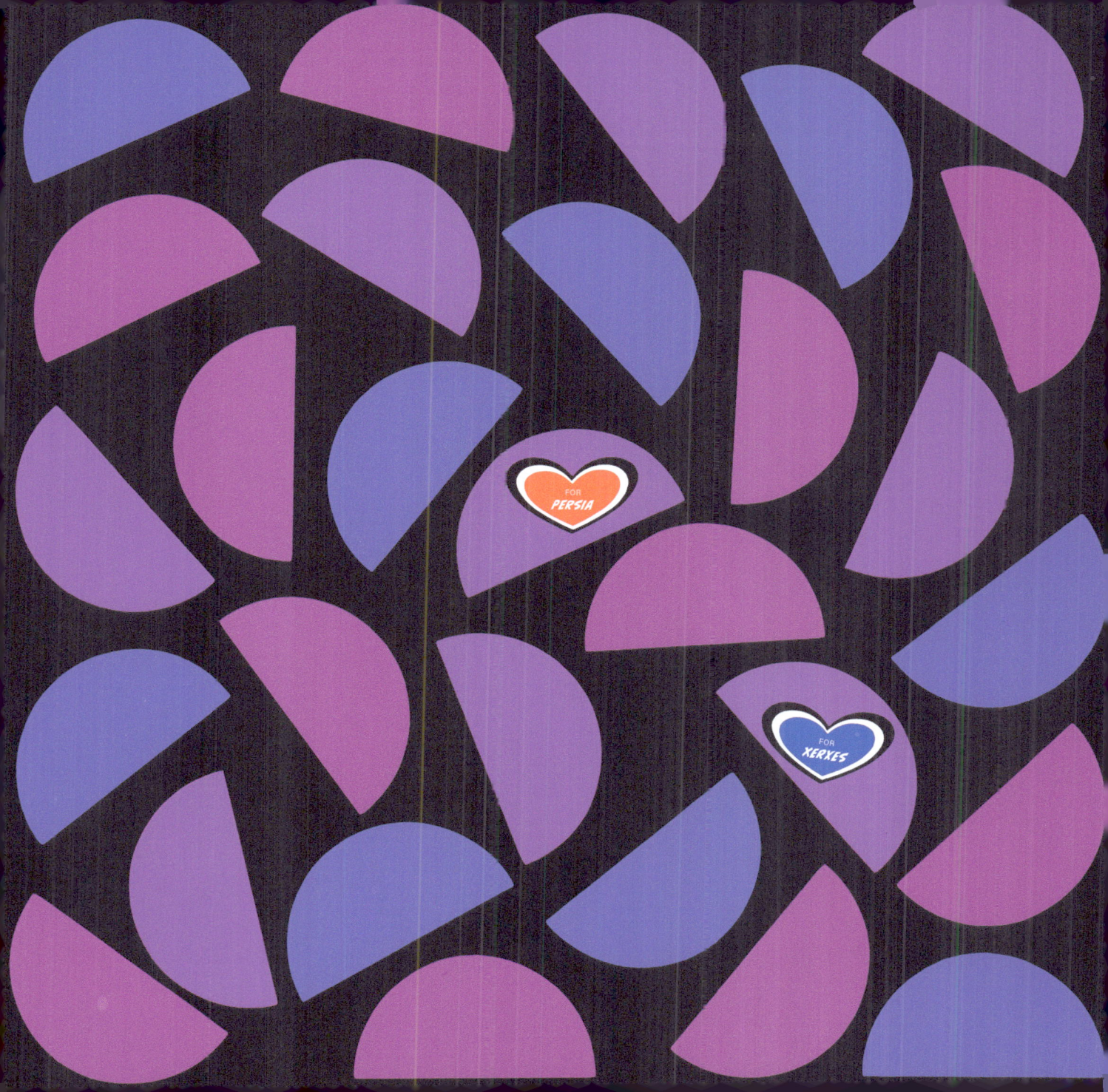

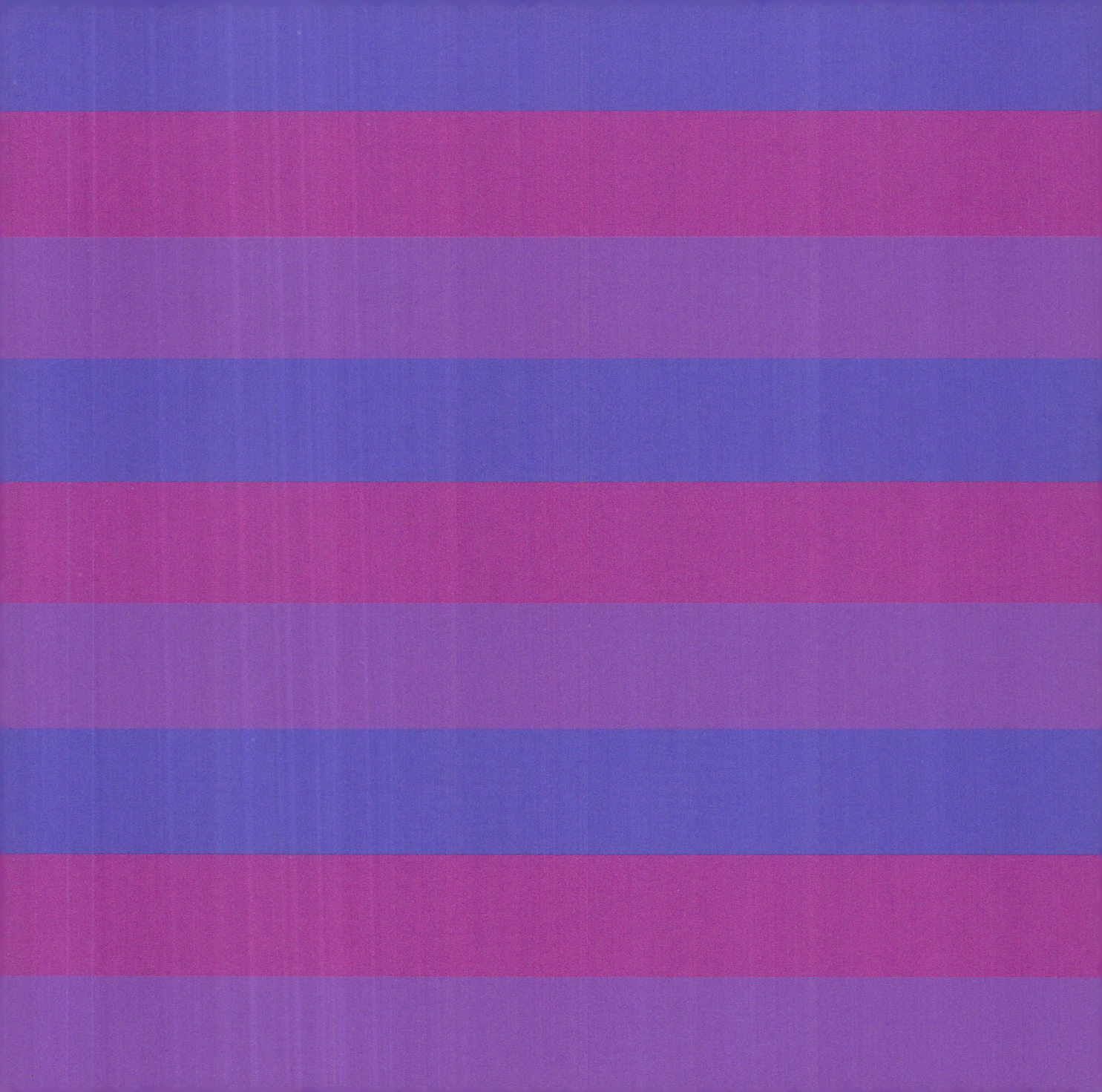

PURPLE

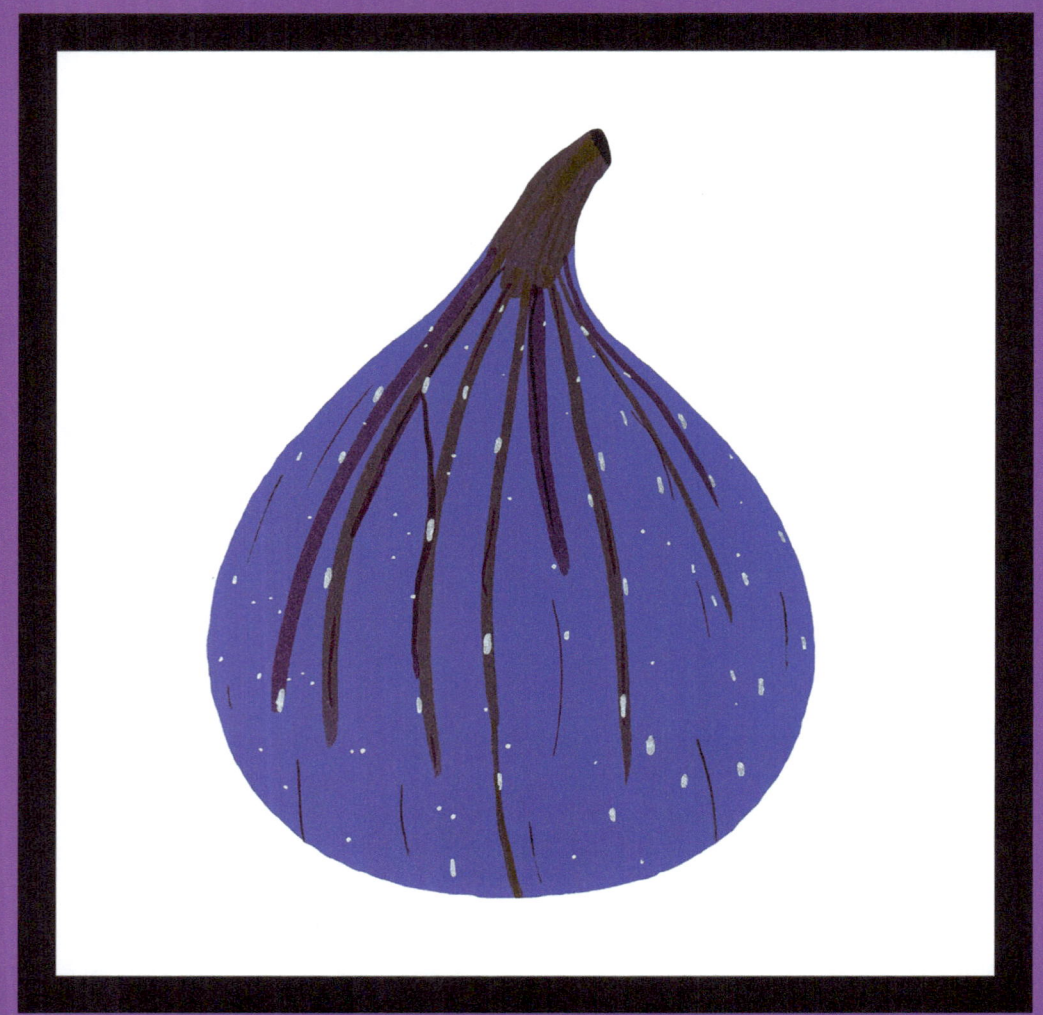

FIGS HAVE BEEN MENTIONED SINCE THE BEGINNING OF TIME...

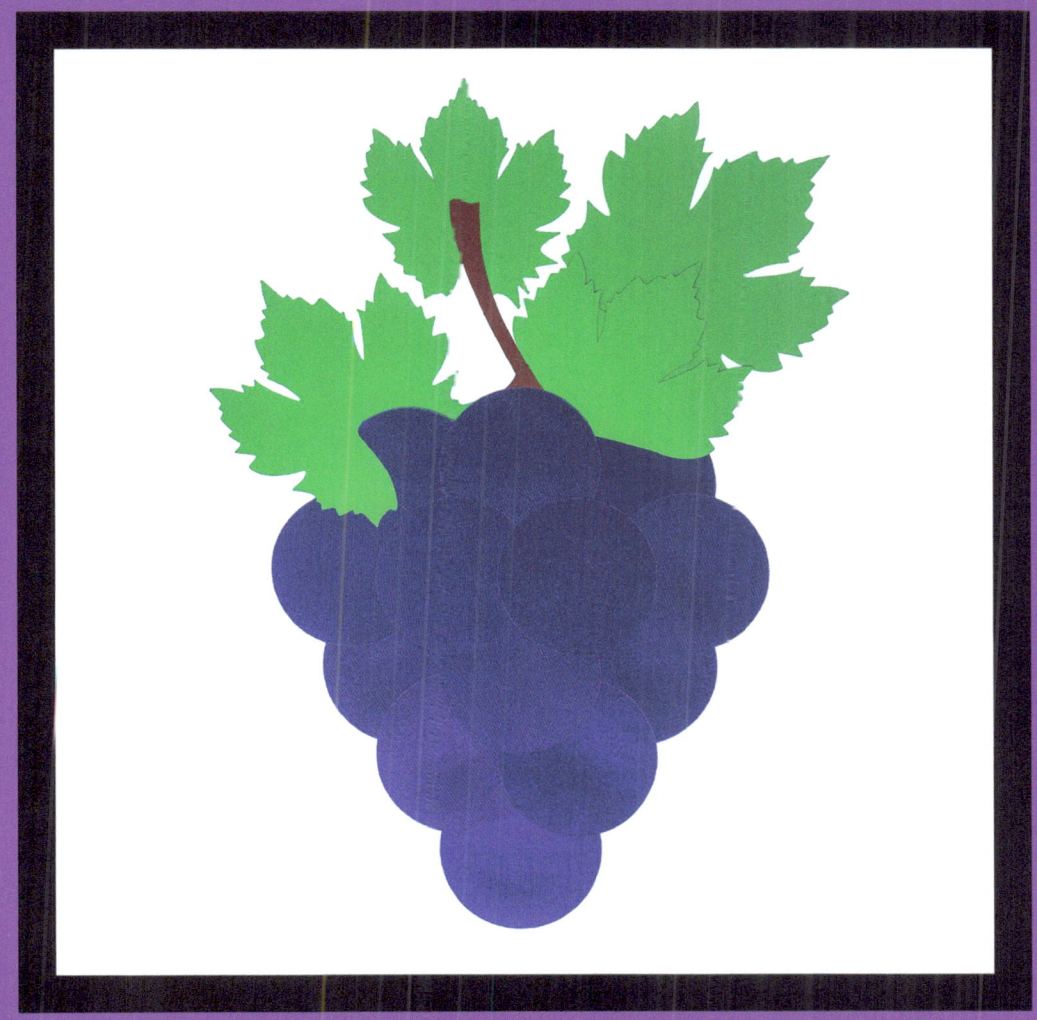

SO HAVE GRAPES THAT ARE TURNED INTO JUICE AND WINE!

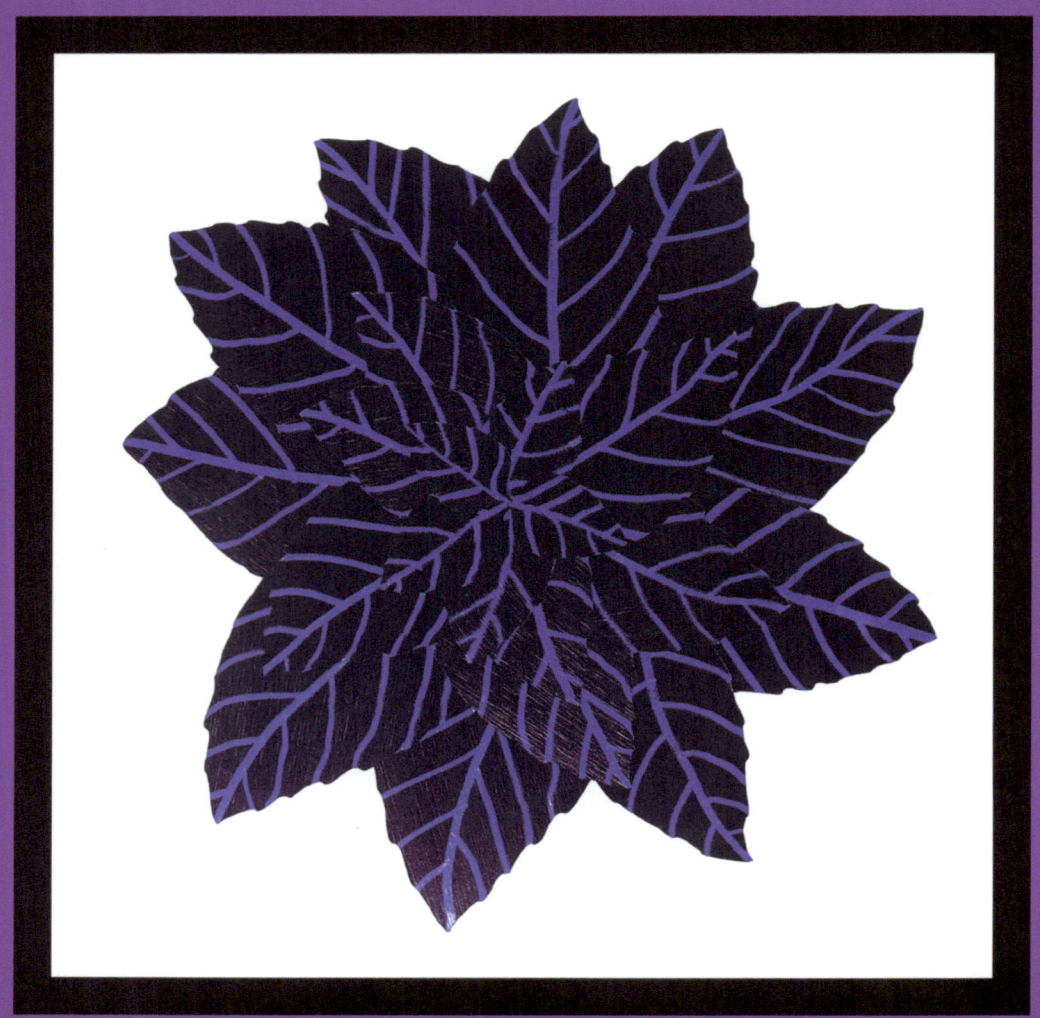

PURPLE BASIL IS AN AWARD-WINNING HERB...

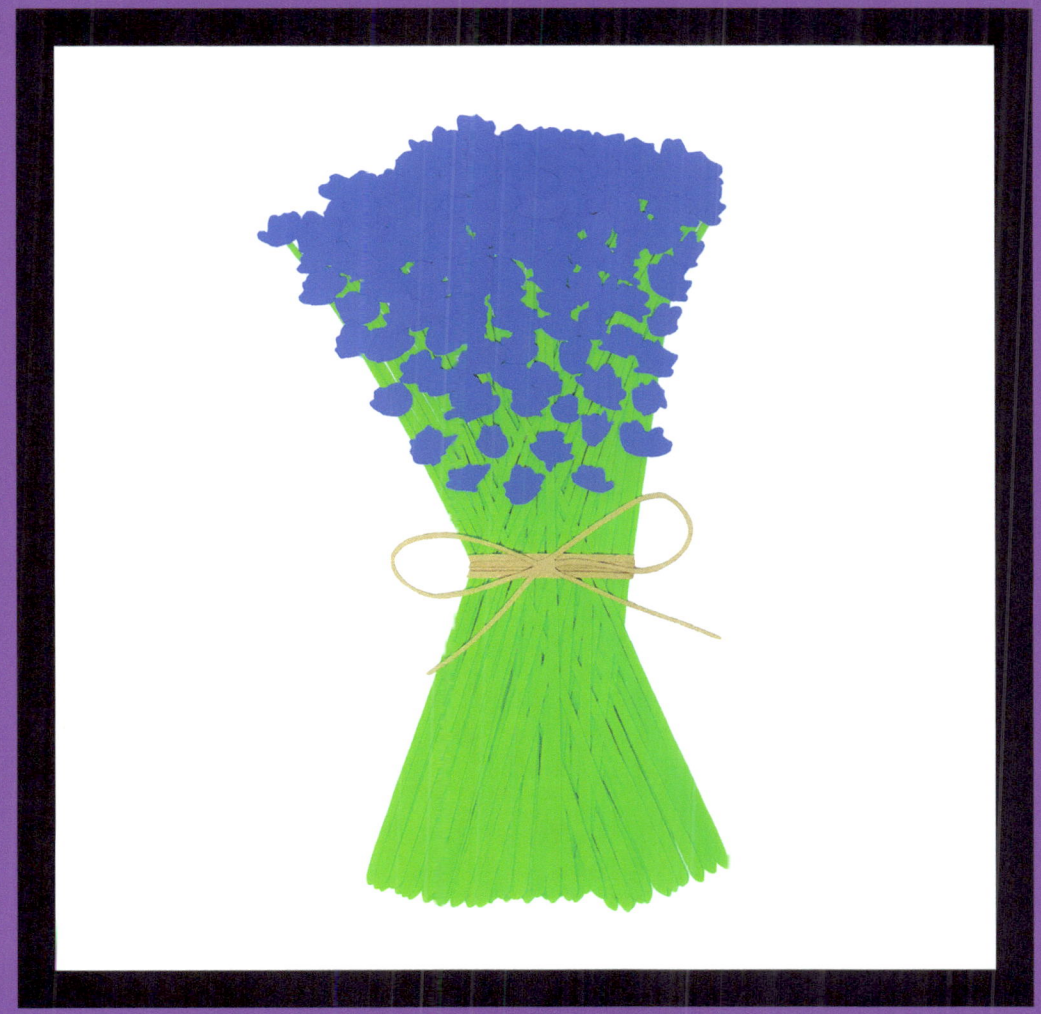

LAVENDER IS ALSO SUPERB!

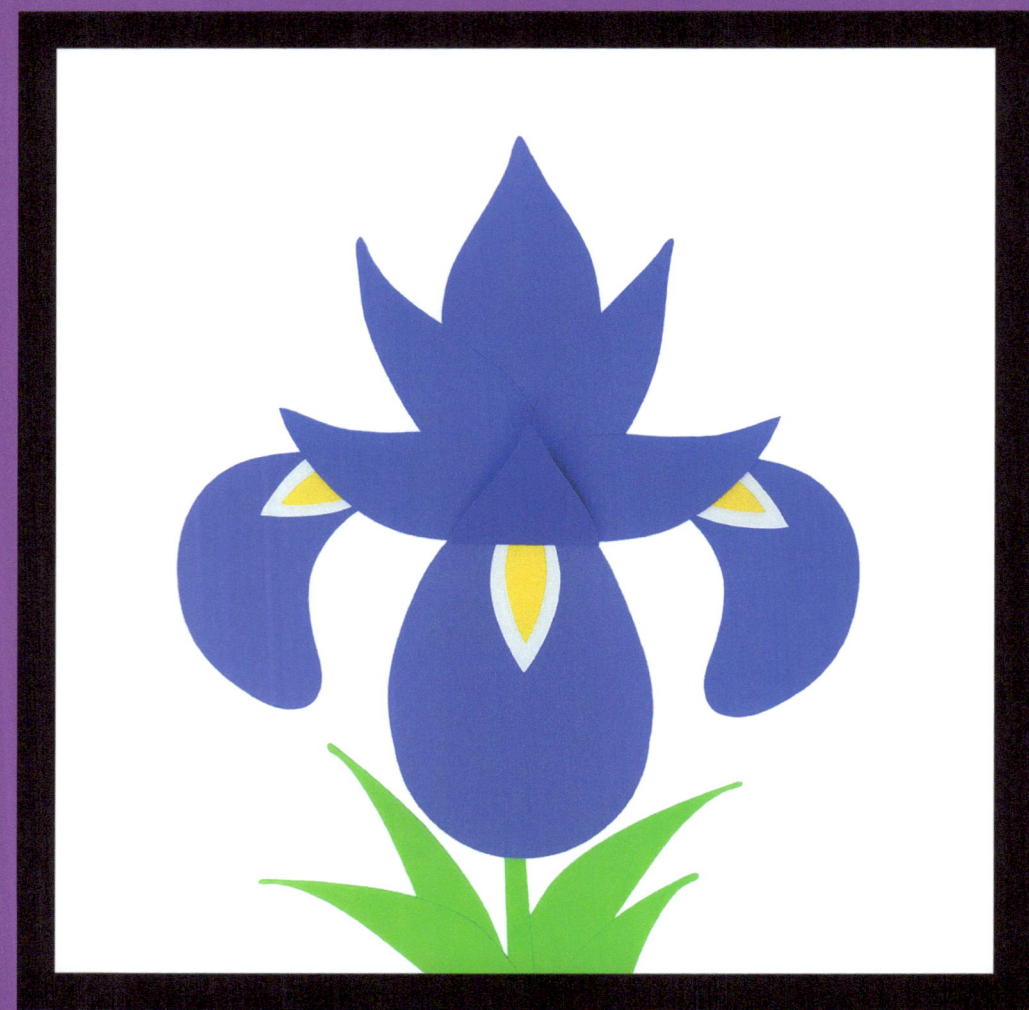

THE IRIS IS A SHOW-STOPPING FLOWER...

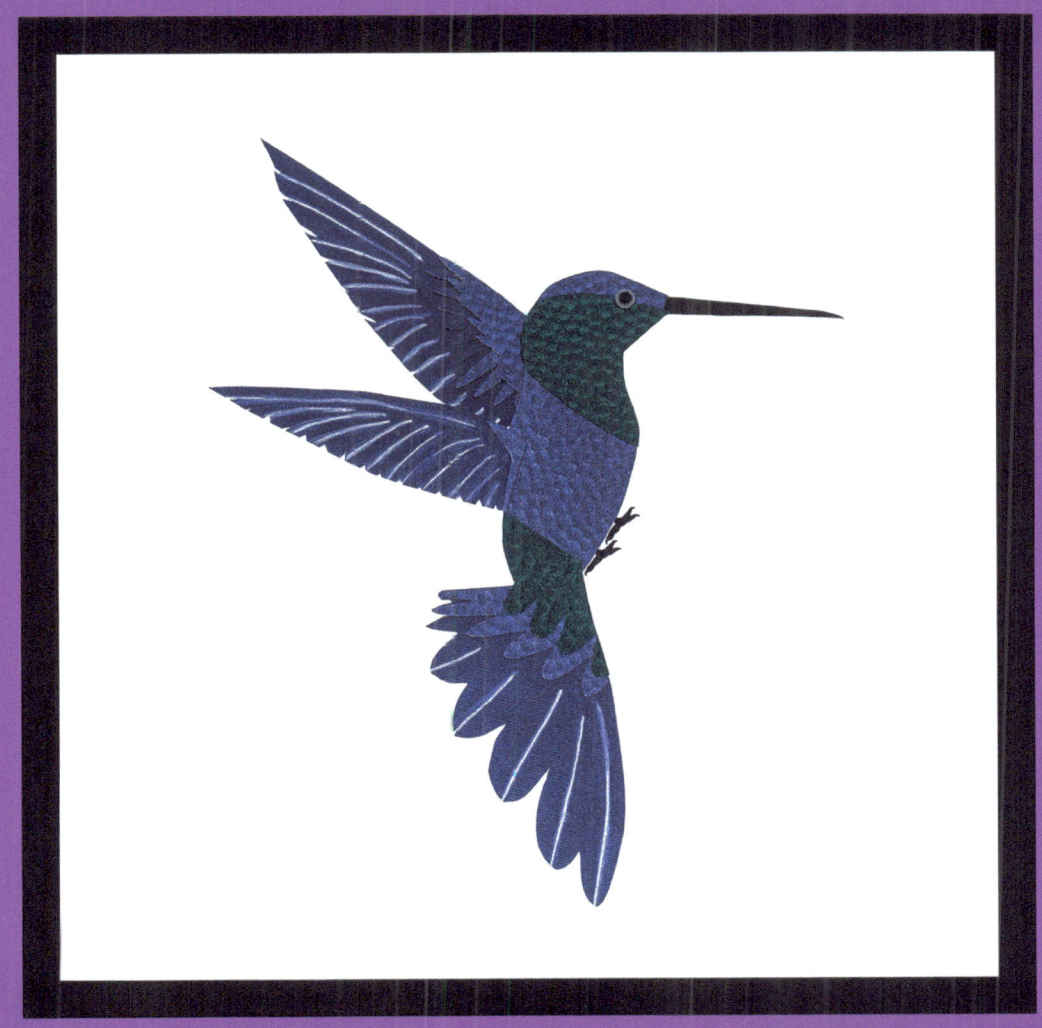

THE VIOLET-CROWNED WOODNYMPH FLIES 60 MILES PER HOUR!

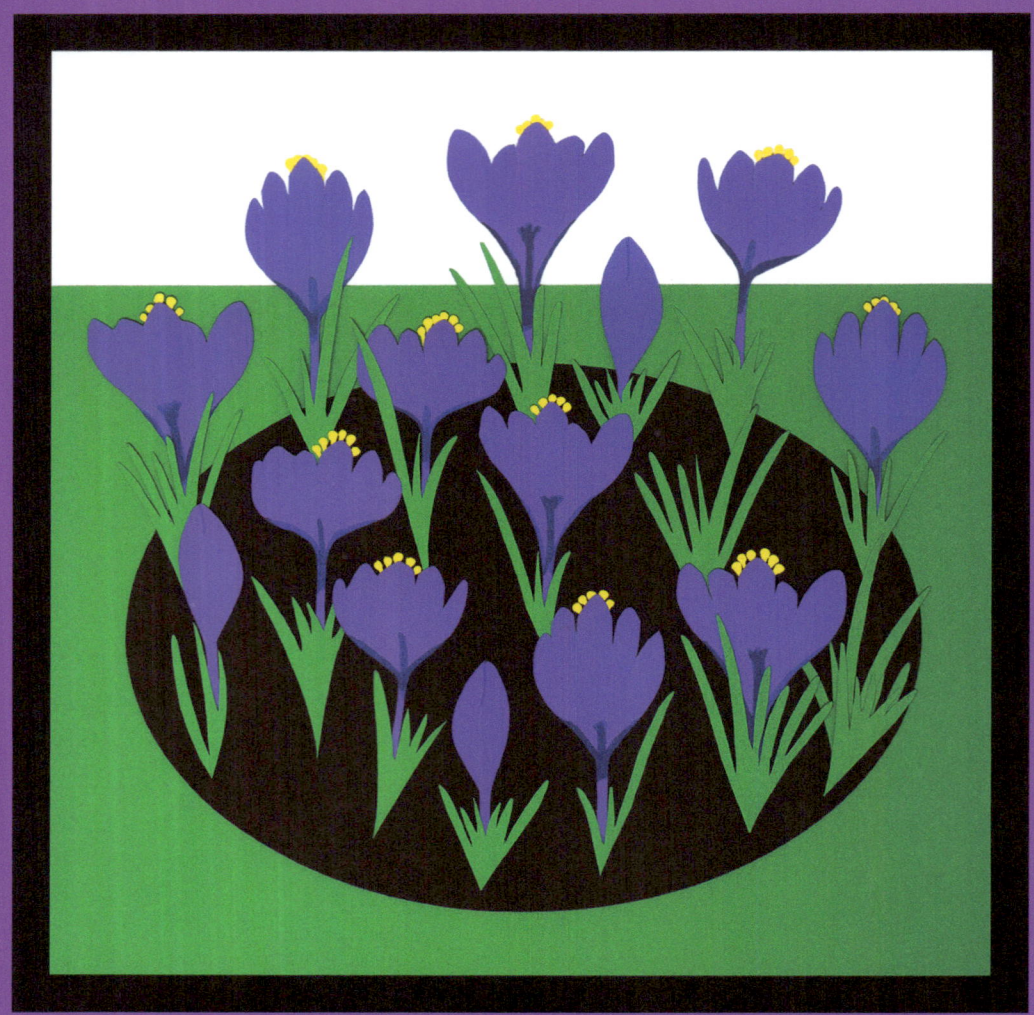

CROCUS FLOWERS APPEAR IN THE SPRING...

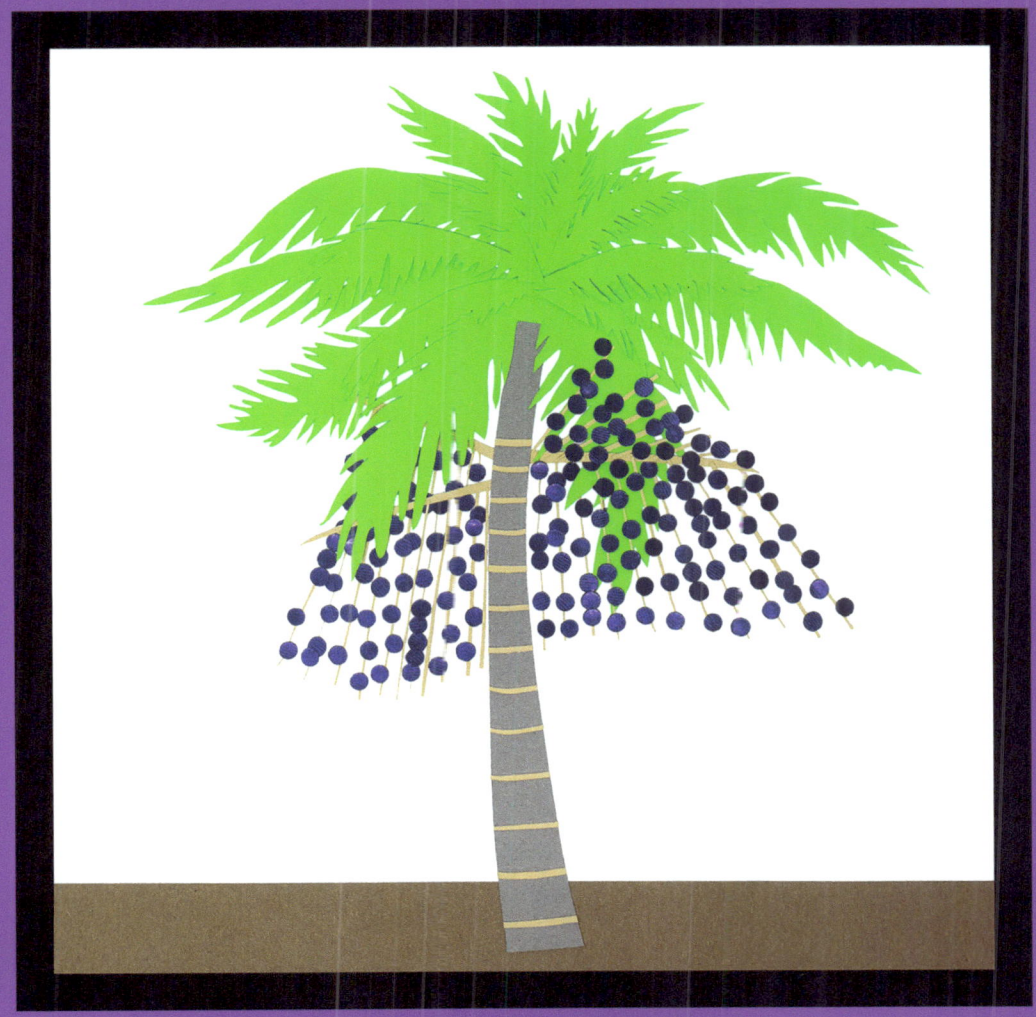

ACAI BERRIES GROW ON BRANCHES THAT LOOK LIKE STRING!

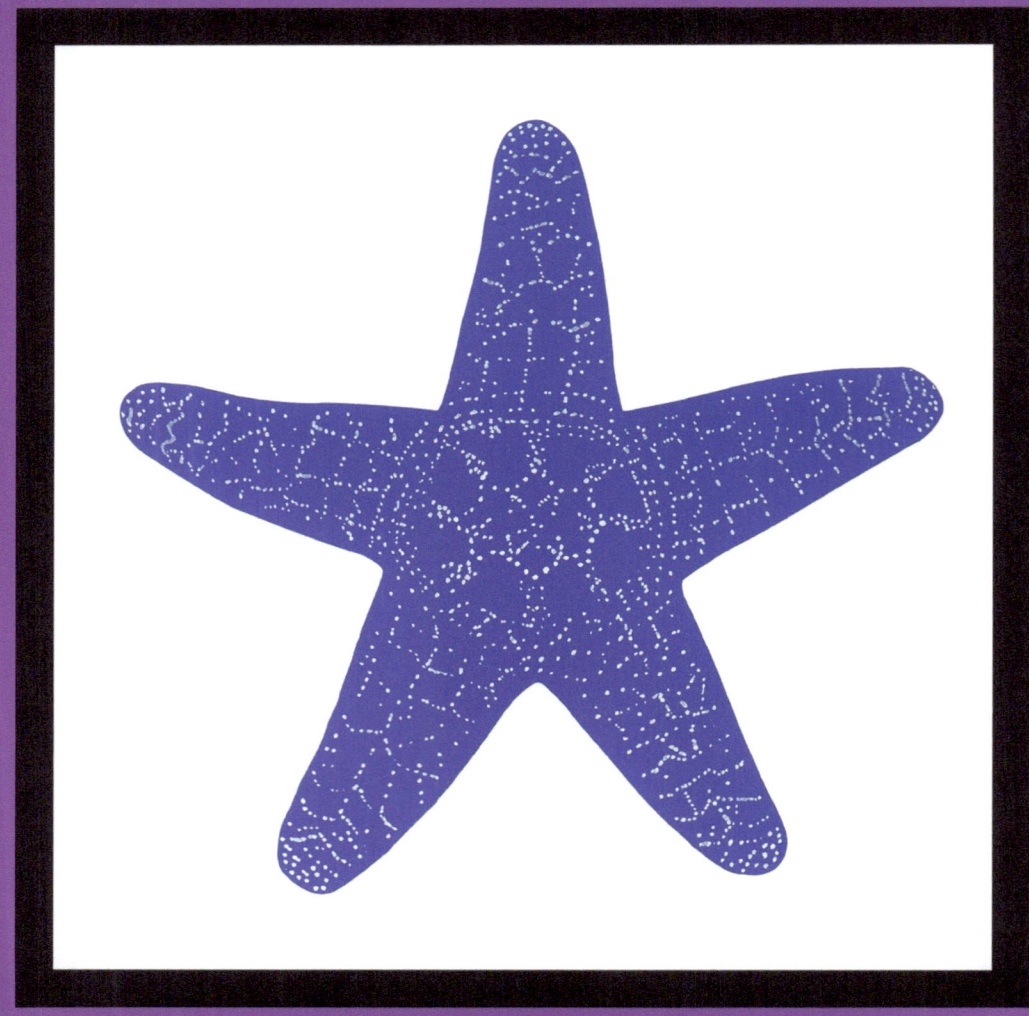

YOU CAN FIND PURPLE STARFISH IN THE PACIFIC OCEAN...

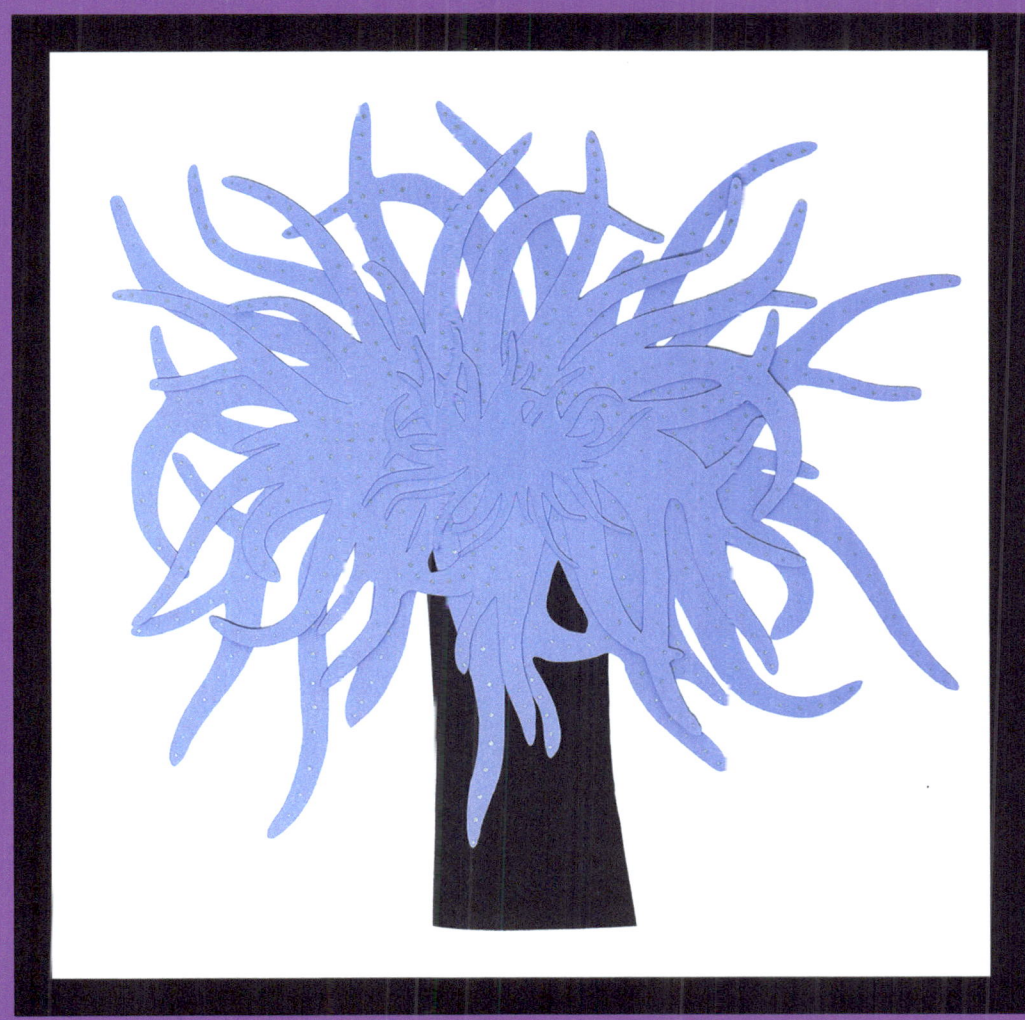

NEAR SEA ANEMONES THAT DANCE WITH FLUID MOTION!

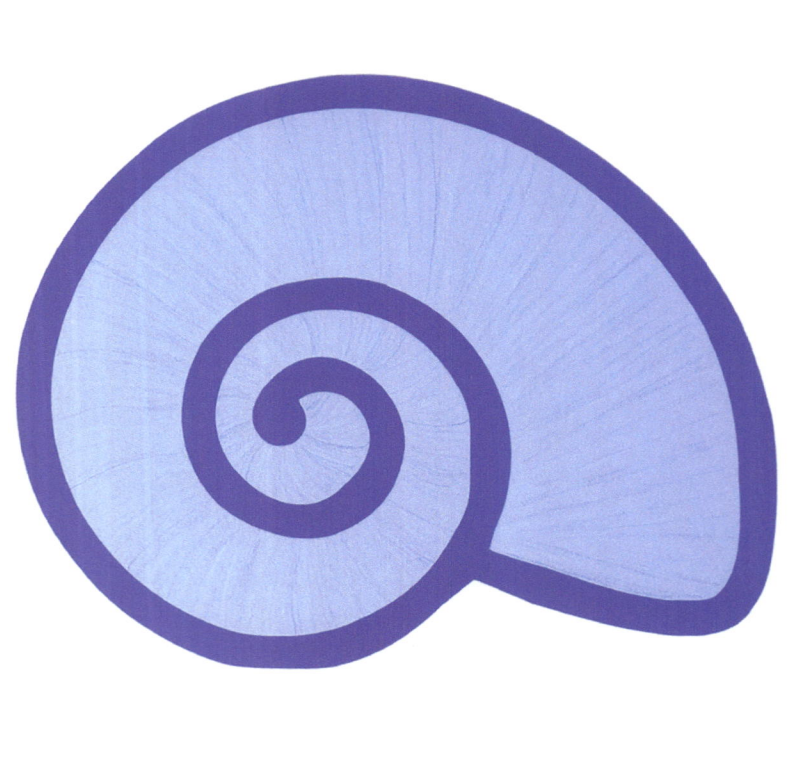

VIOLET SEA SNAILS FLOAT ON THE WATER'S SURFACE...

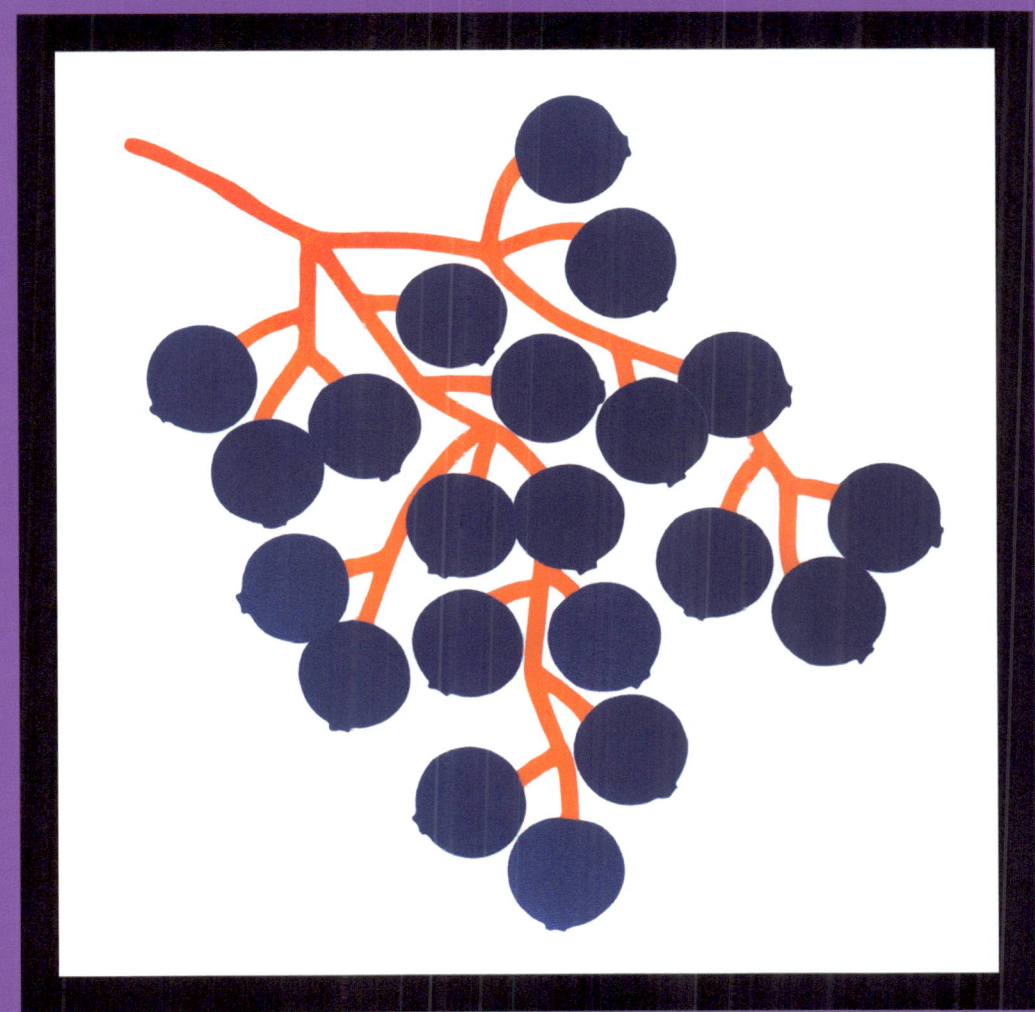

IF YOU NEED ANTIOXIDANTS, ELDERBERRY IS A GOOD PURCHASE!

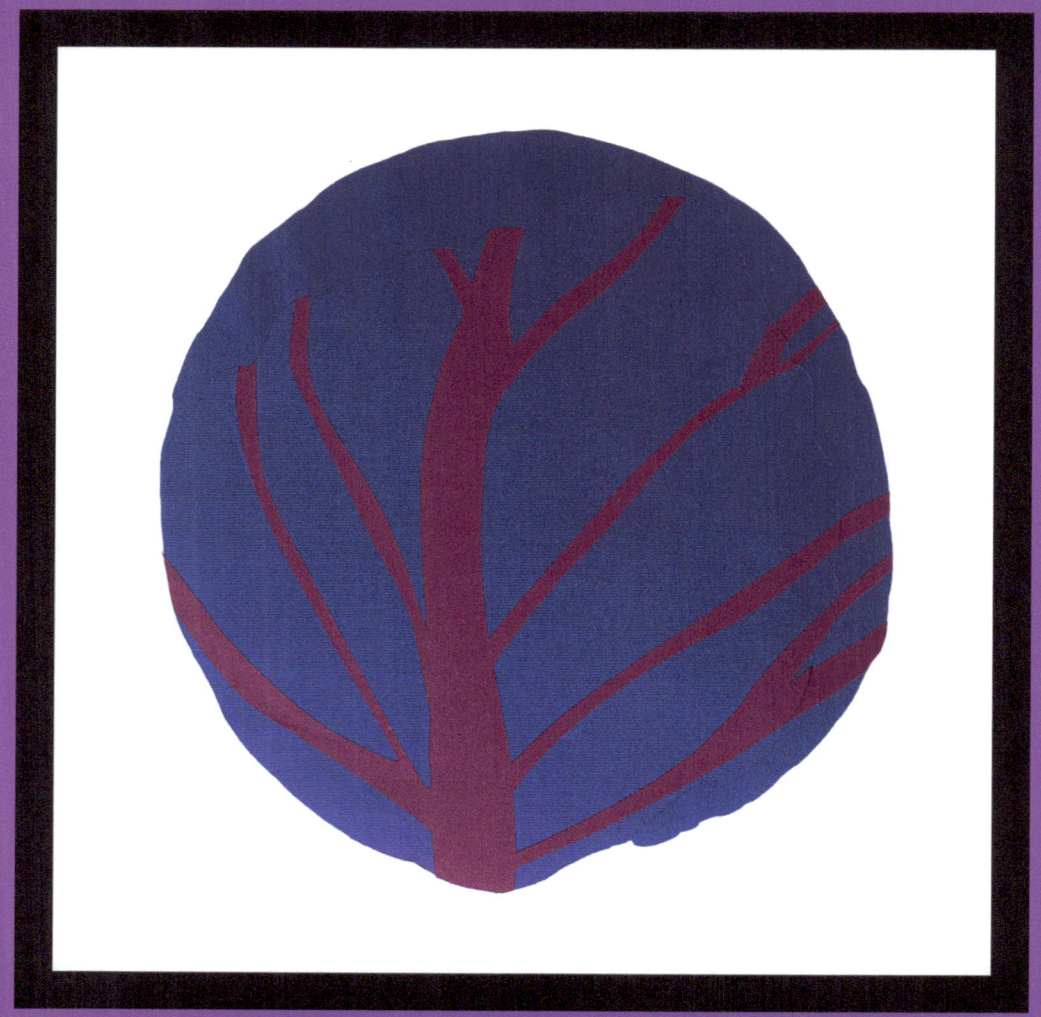

A NOTE IN CONCLUDING OUR GRAND COLOR SPREE:
WHAT WE CALL RED CABBAGE
IS PURPLE, YOU SEE...

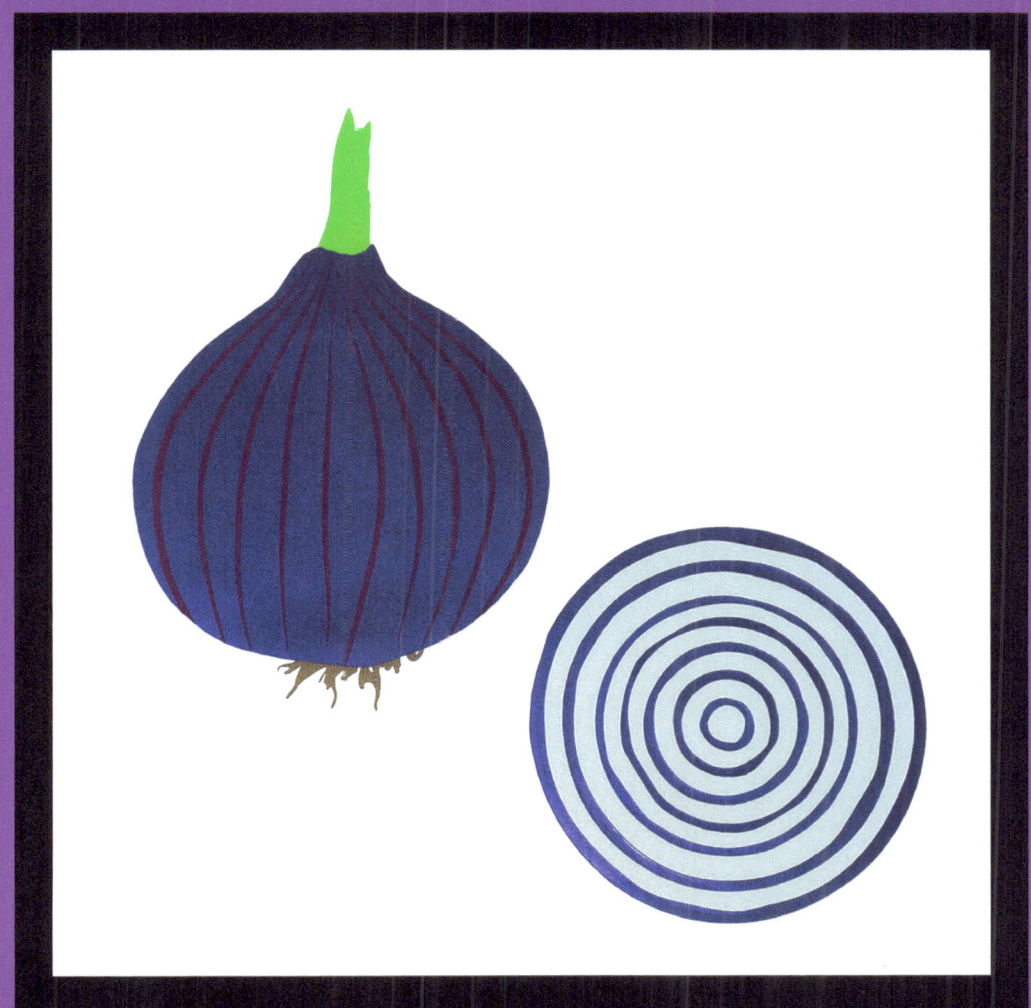

LET'S REVIEW EVERYTHING WITH A PURPLE HUE!

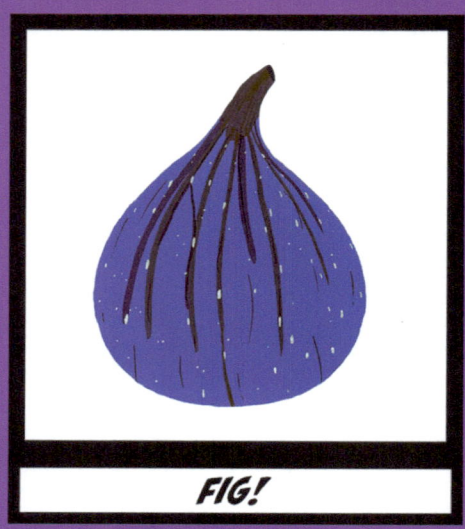

FIG!

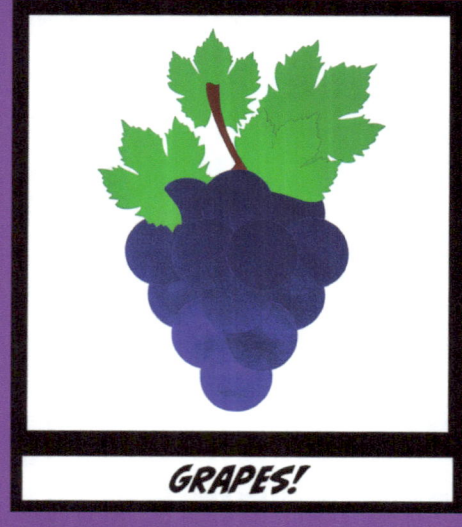

GRAPES!

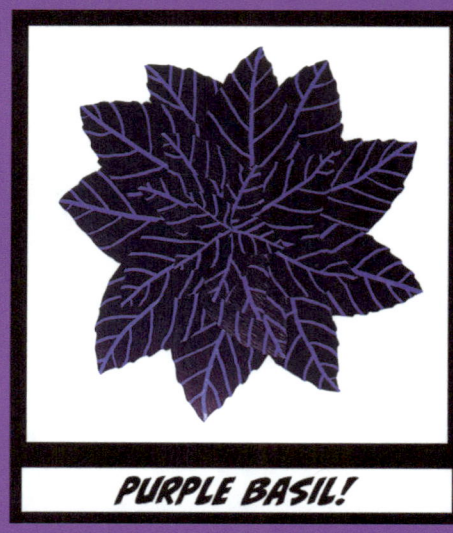

PURPLE BASIL!

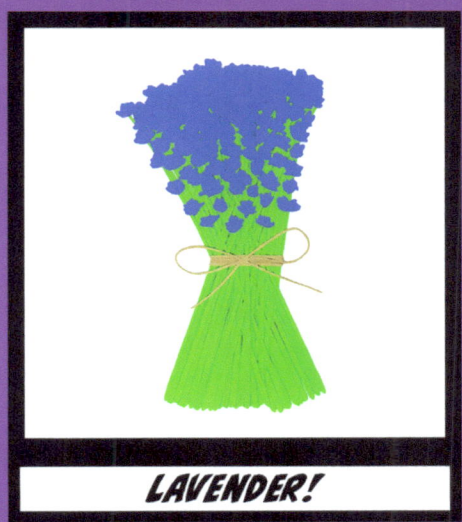
LAVENDER!

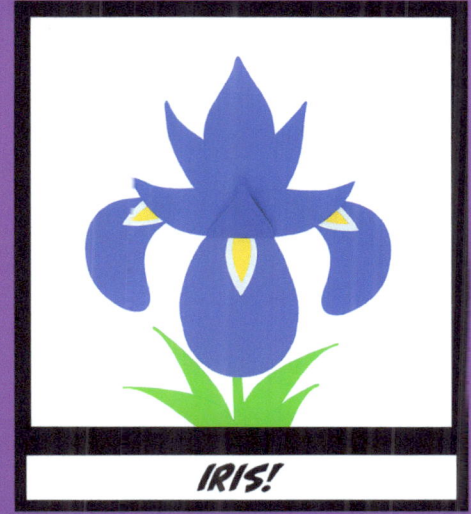
IRIS!

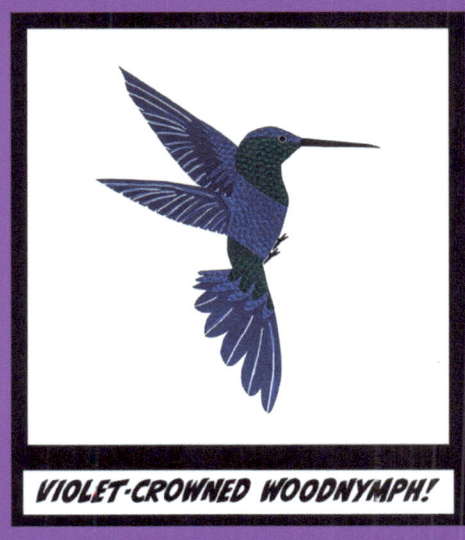
VIOLET-CROWNED WOODNYMPH!

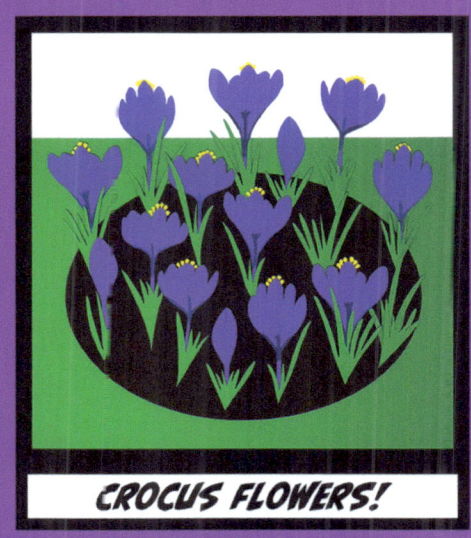
CROCUS FLOWERS!

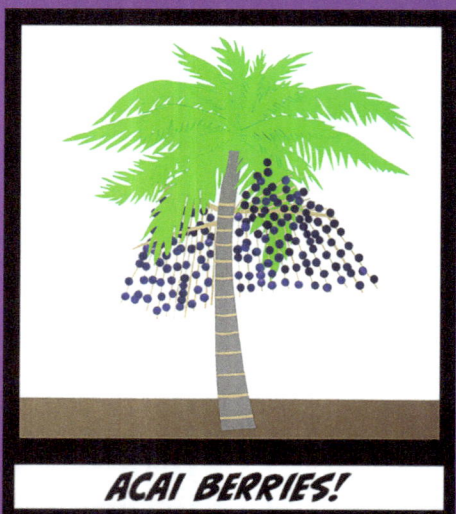
ACAI BERRIES!

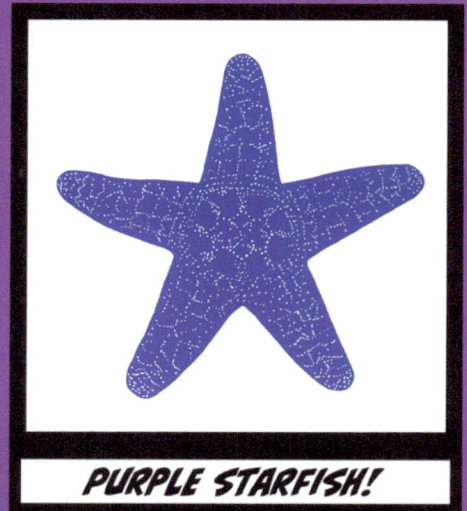
PURPLE STARFISH!

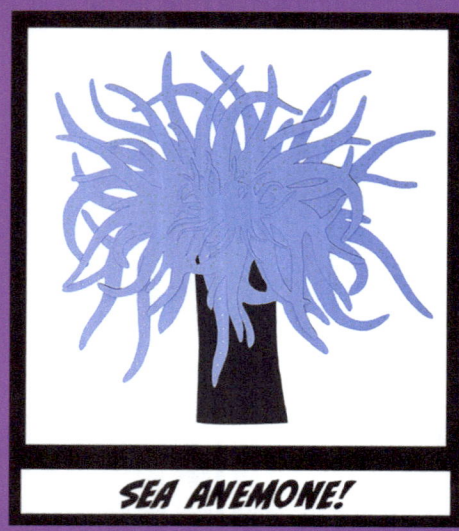
SEA ANEMONE!

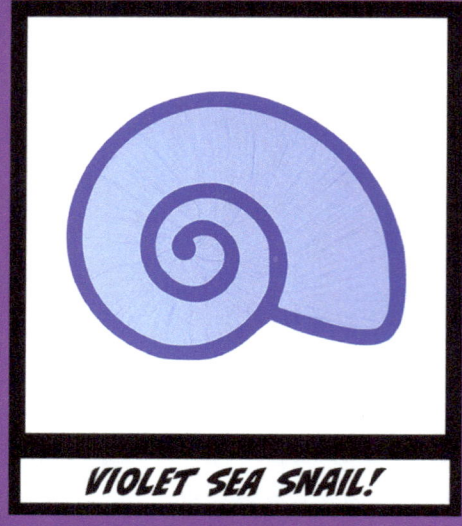
VIOLET SEA SNAIL!

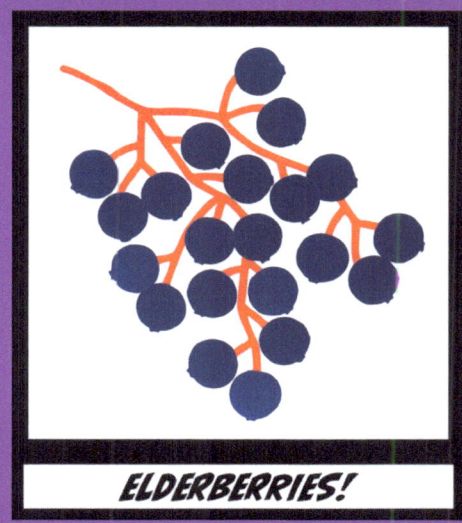
ELDERBERRIES!

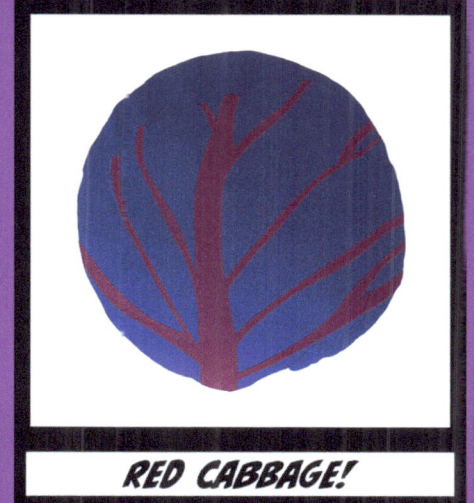
RED CABBAGE!

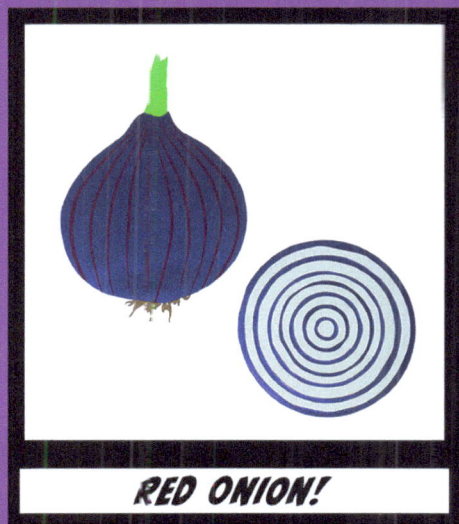
RED ONION!

NICE JOB, AND NOW WE'RE THROUGH. ISN'T IT FUN TO LEARN SOMETHING NEW!

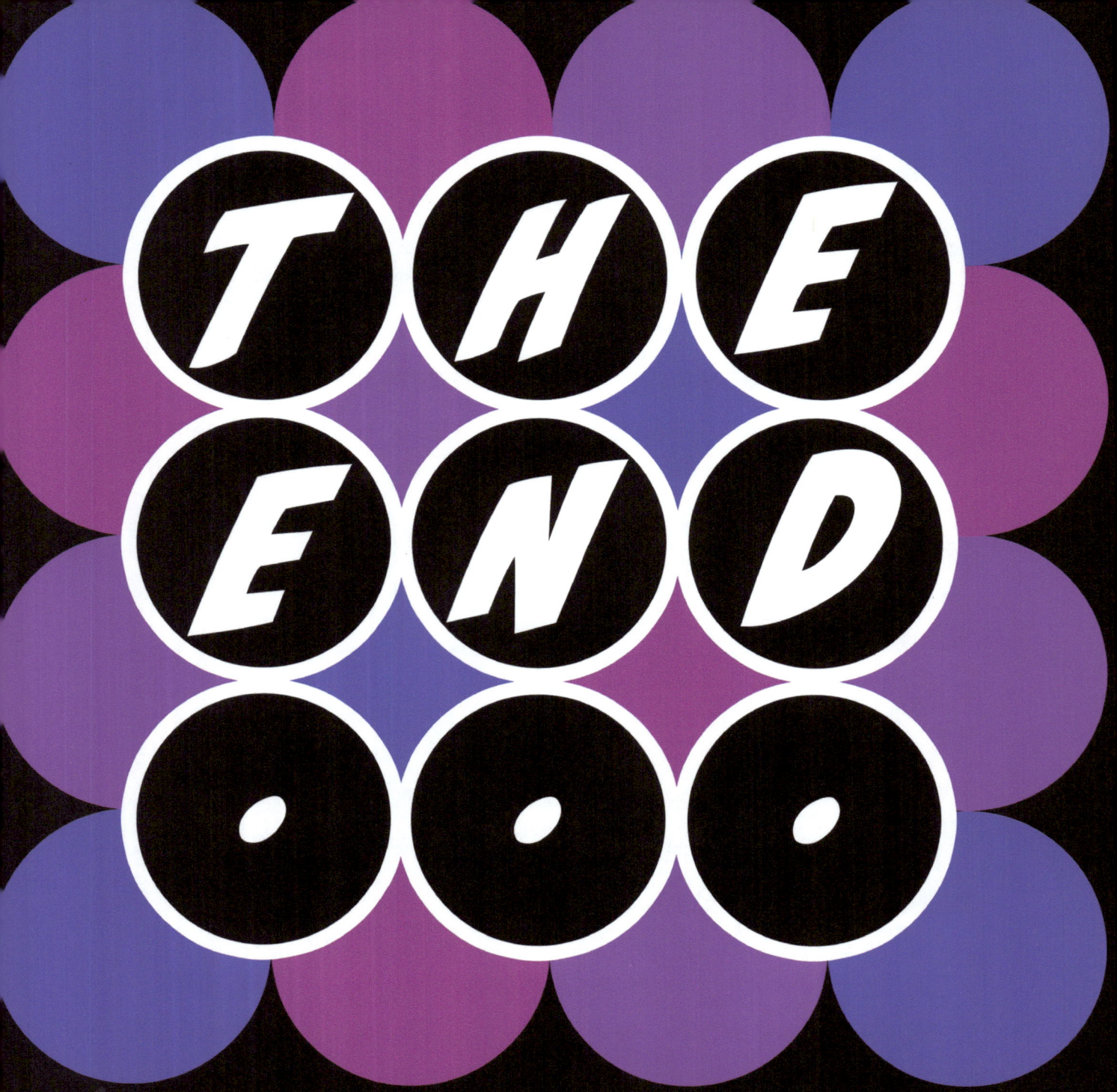

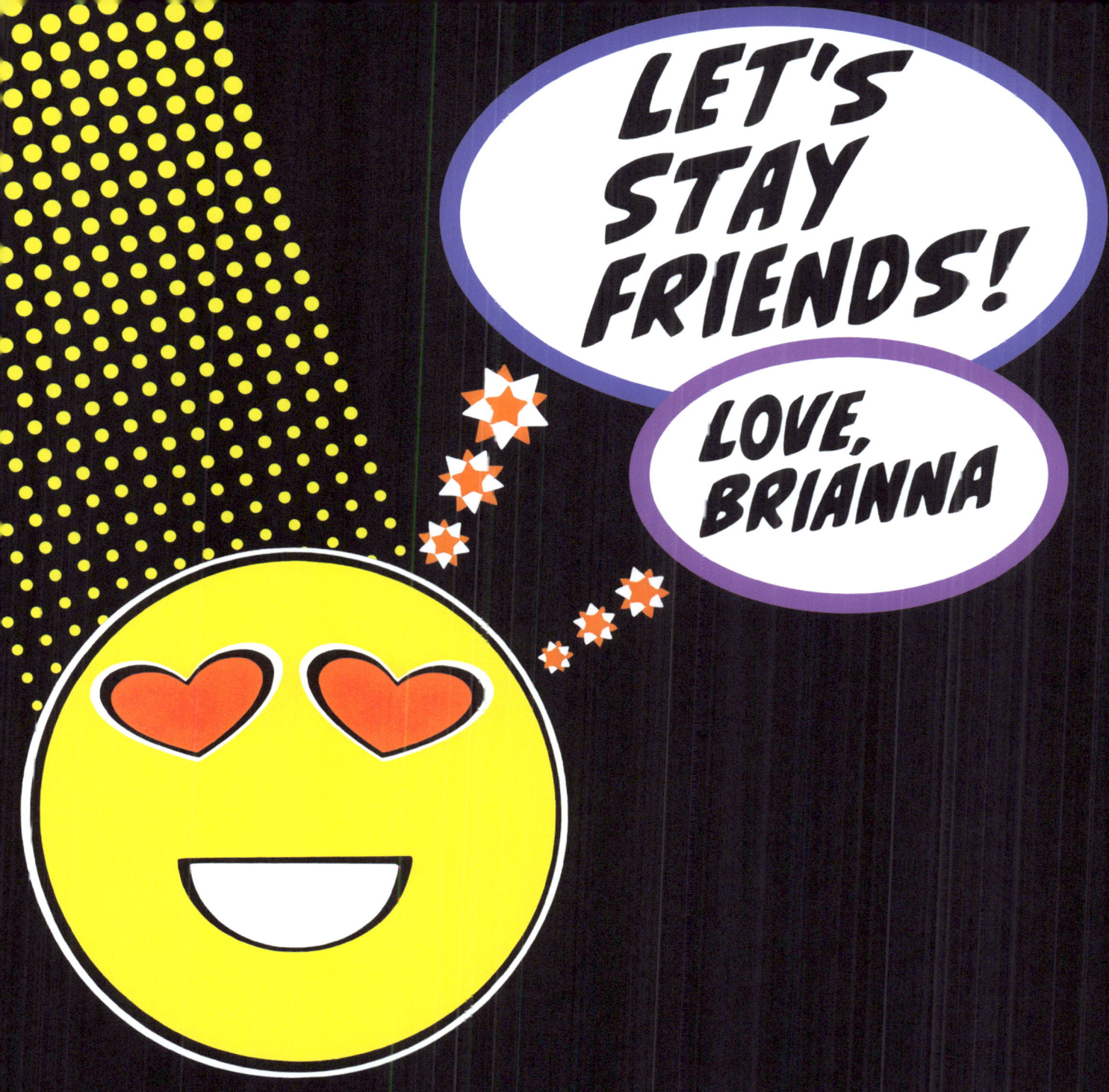

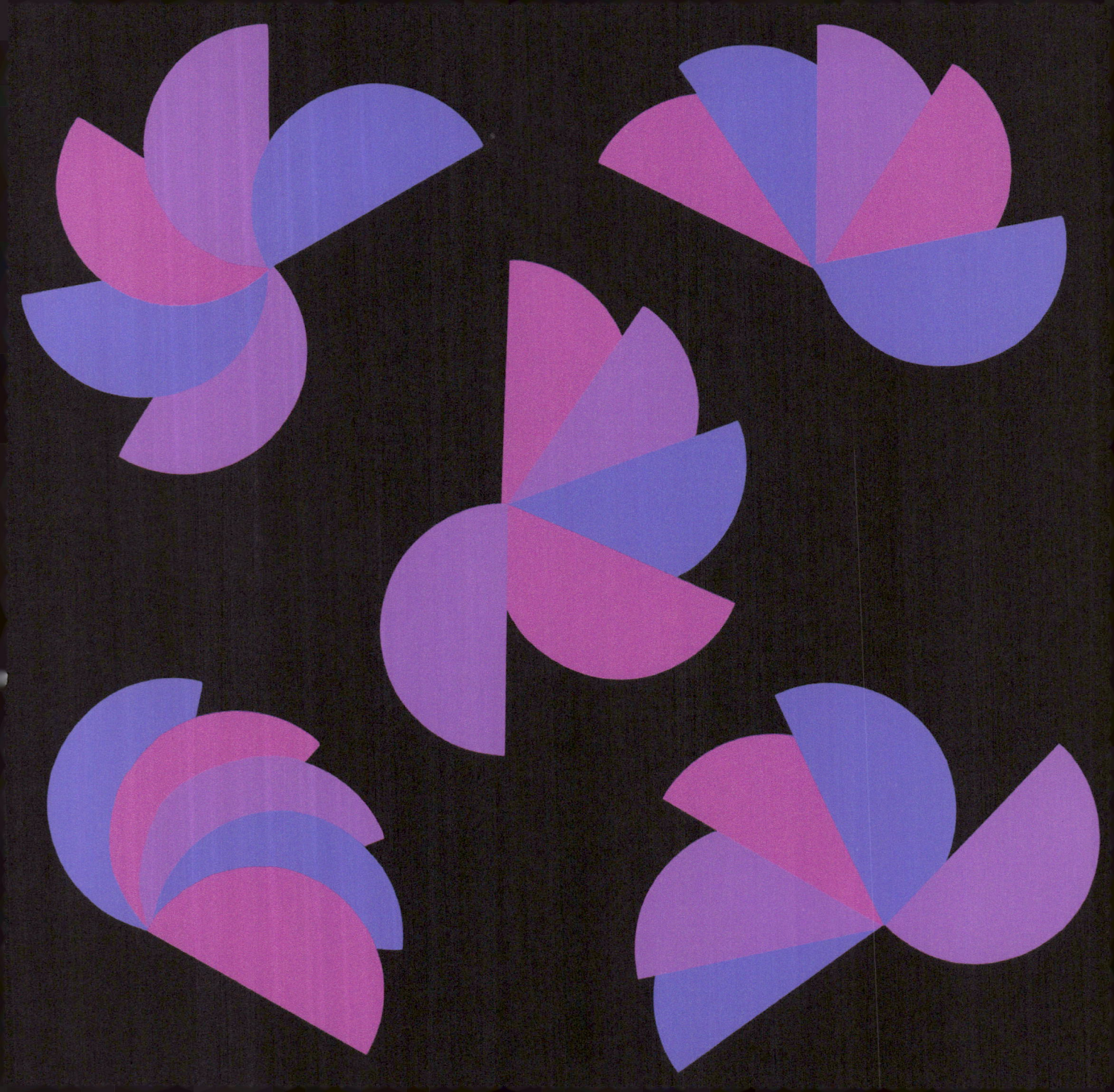

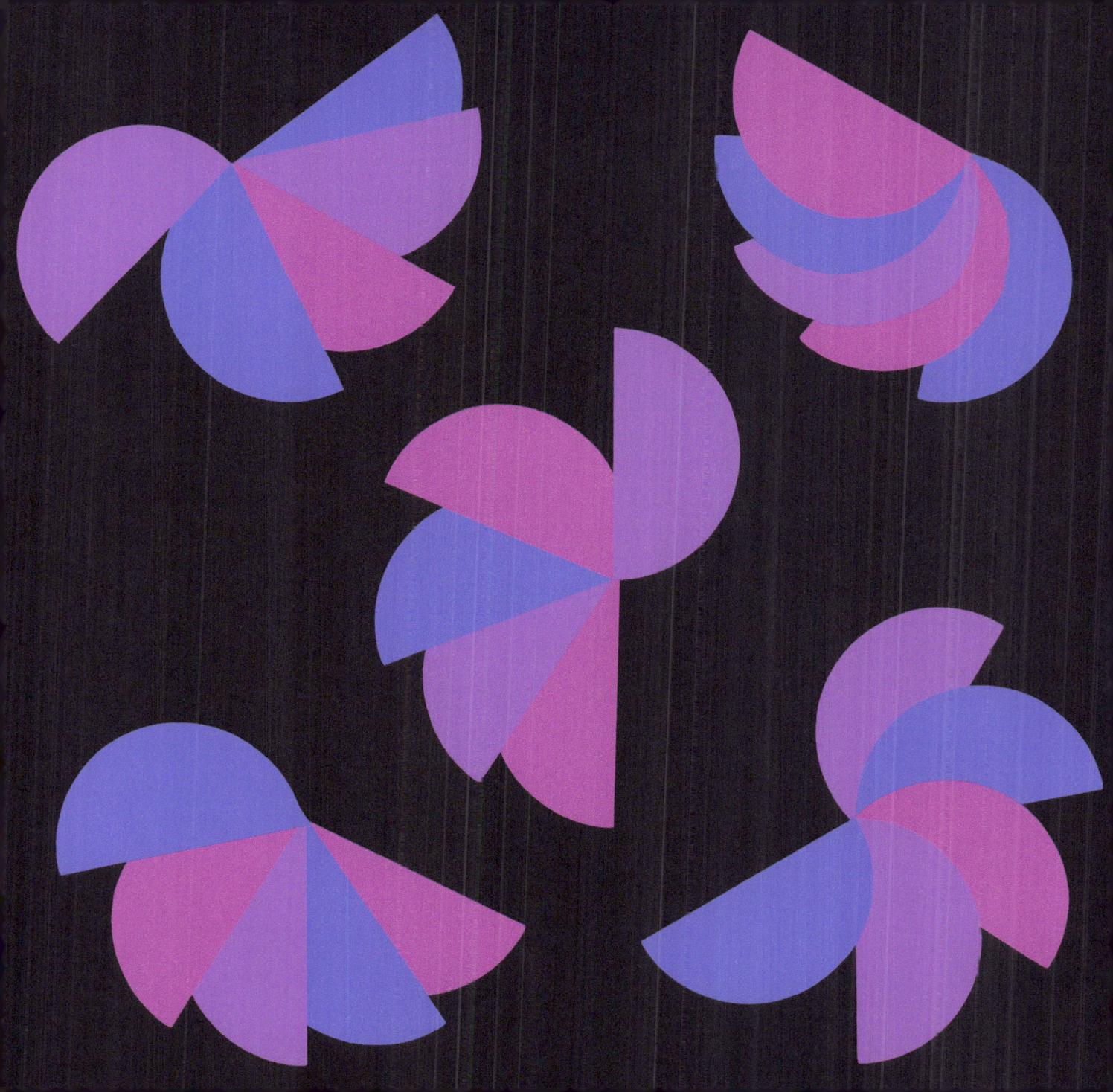

POP ART BOOKs AVAILABLE NOW

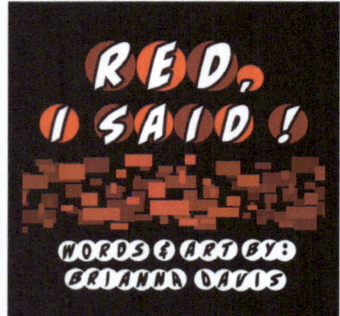
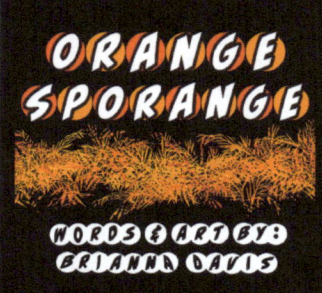
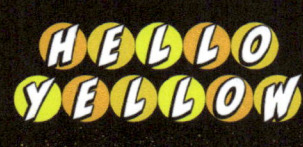
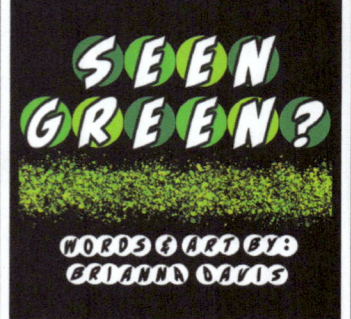
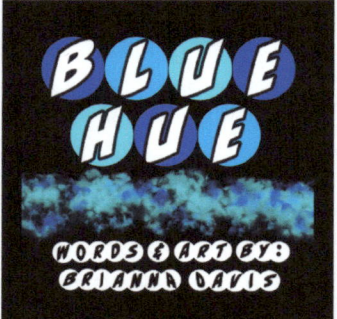
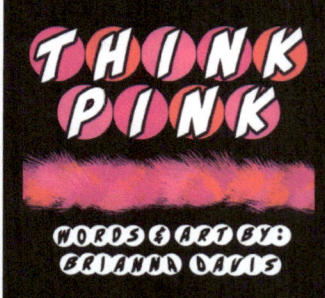
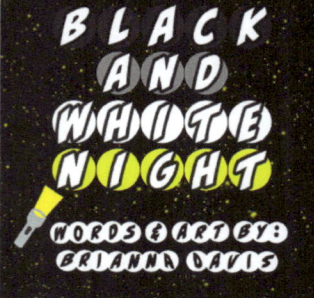
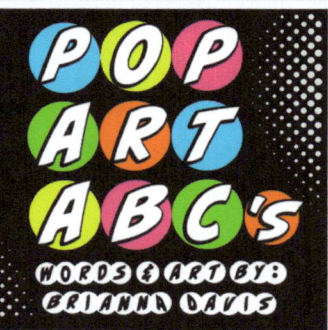
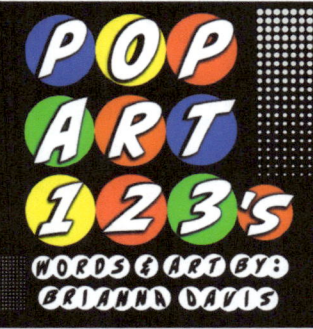

- RED, I SAID! — Words & Art by: Brianna Davis
- ORANGE SPORANGE — Words & Art by: Brianna Davis
- HELLO YELLOW — Words & Art by: Brianna Davis
- SEEN GREEN? — Words & Art by: Brianna Davis
- BLUE HUE — Words & Art by: Brianna Davis
- THINK PINK — Words & Art by: Brianna Davis
- BLACK AND WHITE NIGHT — Words & Art by: Brianna Davis
- POP ART ABC's — Words & Art by: Brianna Davis
- POP ART 123's — Words & Art by: Brianna Davis

www.ingramcontent.com/pod-product-compliance
Lightning Source LLC
Chambersburg PA
CBHW040057250526
45473CB00043B/1800